The Lightning and the Gale

This book is a collection of poems from a former Navy SEAL warrior, drawn from his vast experience and operations around the world, especially in the Western Pacific and Southwest Asia. He also draws extensively from his deep Southern heritage.

Michael R. Howard

La Maison Publishing
Vero Beach, Florida
The Hibiscus City
lamaisonpublishing@gmail.com

"Poetry is the history of the human heart."

Billy Collins

For

Suzanne

Acknowledgments

Grateful acknowledgment is given to publications in which the following poems first appeared:

The Indian River Review - Issue 5 2017 – 2018:
"Breath of the St. John's"

The Porch Writers 2018: "Where the Moss Don't Grow"
"Breath of the St. John's"
"Rock of Remagen"
The Porch Poets – Volume II – April 2019:
"Comanche Dream"

It is a pleasure to acknowledge the help and encouragement of many people who made this book possible. My fellow poets and writers of our Fort Pierce Creative Writer's Group, The Laura Riding Jackson Foundation's Porch Poets and Pole Barn Poets, and my relentless cheerleader Margaret Hawke, all of whom helped make these poems better with their kind suggestions. And more recently, thanks to my Editor Susan Lovelace and Publisher Janet Sierzant, two lovely ladies who made my work far better. Thank you.

Introduction

At the age of twelve, my English teacher tasked us to select, memorize, and recite a poem of our choosing. I haphazardly chose *Old Ironsides* by Oliver Wendell Holmes, Sr. The subject, rhythm, and cadence, and its impact on the public at that time made such an impression on me that I became enthralled with poetry. I can still recite that poem today and included it in this book with several other favorite poems. I hope some are familiar to you.

The last line of the *Old Ironsides* poem is the title of this book. I've long held a fascination with this ship, the *USS Constitution*, one of our nation's first naval warships and one that remains a commissioned ship today with an active Navy crew. It is a beautiful ship that speaks to those adventurous tall ship sailing days when the world was large. As a Navy Captain, I was once piped aboard the USS Constitution where she was moored in Boston harbor, an honor I would have received upon boarding any current Navy warship. It was unexpected, but thrilling, and followed by an extensive tour of the ship, where I was privileged to see what remains of the original ship. It felt like seeing the sacred bones of some great historical figure. The book title honors that ship and the poem that saved it.

The cover art is part of the woodblock print by the Japanese artist Hokusai. It is *The Great Wave off Kanagawa*, published in 1831. The image depicts huge waves threatening several boats as Mount Fuji looms in the background. I climbed Mount Fuji in 1985, a magical experience. I can identify with the men in these boats as they work together as a tight-knit team to survive and negotiate these enormous waves. I've been there and done that. I am intrigued by Hokusai's print and wanted to share it as part of my book.

The notes at the end are there to help with context should you choose to use them. But I also hope you find additional things within the poems that impact you in some visceral way. I would feel satisfied and successful if one poem in this collection elicited a simple emotion in you. If you feel a twinge of something when you read one of these poems, perhaps I've done my job. I hope you enjoy this collection.

Contents

Old Ironsides

By Oliver Wendell Holmes, Sr.

Ay, tear her tattered ensign down!
    Long has it waved on high,
And many an eye has danced to see
    That banner in the sky;
Beneath it rung the battle shout,
    And burst the cannon's roar; —
The meteor of the ocean air
    Shall sweep the clouds no more.

Her deck, once red with heroes' blood,
    Where knelt the vanquished foe,
When winds were hurrying o'er the flood,
    And waves were white below,
No more shall feel the victor's tread,
    Or know the conquered knee; —
The harpies of the shore shall pluck
    The eagle of the sea!

Oh, better that her shattered hulk
    Should sink beneath the wave;
Her thunders shook the mighty deep,
    And there should be her grave;
Nail to the mast her holy flag,
    Set every threadbare sail,
And give her to the god of storms,
    The lightning and the gale!

My Dhow

I will take you home,
My Dhow,
And sail you along my genteel coast,
As rare a sight could be indeed,
Bumping, shouldering against The Stream.

I will walk your salt-cured decks
Where so many knelt in prayer.
Sand and caulk your weathered planks
And clean the Asian borers
From your ancient hull.

My Dhow, who in centuries past
Plied Zanzibar's lurid coast,
Will now scour our Golden Isles,
Our Treasure Coast,
Where sunken galleons look up
From watery graves with envy.

What shall I carry below
In your ample holds,
Once laden with dates, fish,
And slaves? You labored with grace,
Slid with silent ease past the Shat al-Arab,
Lateen sails astrain, friend and foe astride.

Together, we'll trade your Persian Gulf for ours,
Our nor'easter for your monsoon.

And your wind will be mine,
Mine yours, freely blown,
Your waters, mine, and mine yours.
Salt, dry on your decks, the same
On your tongue as mine.
We will sail the same night skies,
Measure the same stars,
Lift together the same sun and moon.

And though neither of us have yet seen
The Southern Cross.
We will find it together,
My Dhow.

High in the Hindu Kush

High our warriors fly into the Hindu Kush,
Where empires go to die.
And through the Khyber Pass they push,
Where many brave soldiers lie.

Rest easy in your graves, old mates.
They'll join you all too soon.
Their flight will not be going home,
Beside you, they'll soon need room.

This is their fight, this day, this age.
They've run to the sound of guns.
Now their helo strains to reach the heights,
From death, they will not run.

This deadly trade, they sought it long.
They're now blessed and cursed with war.
Their youth has made them hard and strong.
Now higher and higher they soar.

High into the thin, cold air they climb,
Ahead, four mates have called for aid.
In grave peril, their fight they'll find,
All deaths will be repaid.

Four mates betrayed this tragic night,
By a simple shepherd's find.
Now they fight in the growing light:

Young lives, all on the line.

Who sent our brave young four, we ask?
But it's too late to question why,
As the cold bites hard in the Hindu Kush sky.
It is their time to die.

They pray their mates will hold their ground.
They pray they'll get there in time.
They bring their vengeance and killing rounds,
And higher and higher they climb.

But fortune favors them not this night,
And fate takes hold their hand.
Just one lives through this dreadful fight,
For the others, it's their last stand.

One final look into each other's eyes,
A thought of loved ones back home.
Their sacred bond holds no lies,
No warrior goes down alone.

Skilled pilots took them in
To the high peaks of the Hindu Kush.
There our brothers shared a fate,
Then morning light brought its hush.

Into the Hindu Kush they fell.
Their warrior spirits freed.
Their SEAL ethos rings clear in every ear,
But their tomorrows will never be.

Rock of Remagen

It held up a bridge
Of great importance once.
Worthy of youthful blood
Which ran in rivulets
Into deep, cold waters,
Under the Remagen Bridge.

Witness to peaceful crossings:
Greetings, handshakes, friendly nods.
Royal, strong - sadly strategic.
Where enemies clashed,
The victors took it from
Under the Remagen Bridge.

Christened by war,
Indifferent to flags and colors,
Battered, scarred,
Burned and blackened,
But cleansed by neutral waters,
Under the Remagen Bridge.
- - -
Now, on patient display
In a lonely, untraveled place.
Neglected, rained on, ignored.
An old tiger in a failing zoo.
No longer holding up,
The bridge at Remagen.

Brass words, dulled by age
Tell vaguely of faded glory.
While new words speak,
"An odd stone, an odd place.
It should be holding up
The bridge at Remagen."

Lay your hand
On the rock from Remagen.
Feel its fading heat
Left now by a setting sun.
No longer warmed by
The burning bridge at Remagen.

It's a seat now for the old, the weary.
A step for the young,
To see further through the trees,
And over the far hill.
Perhaps they'll see
The Rock of Remagen.

A Walk Through Oradour

I walk through old Oradour.
Steps reverent, measured,
Words whispered.
A white fog rises, ghostlike,
From the peaceful, silent river,
Filling vacant frames of homes, shops,
The church, whose blood-stained stones
Gleam again with undeserved innocence.

I reflect on this cool, fall day
And clearly see the choking smoke
That filled every empty street,
Swirled through every
Roof, window, door.
My autumn chill warmed by
Your long-ago fires that sear
My hands, my face, my soul, and burned
Your village white hot with hate.

A crush of red gravel beneath my feet
On your manicured street:
Is this the echo of your
Carbon burned bones when
Jackbooted murderers marched,
Herded you to your fate,
Choreographed your death?
Choreograph, not a word for dying,
Not for massacre of innocents in a church.

I cover my ears
From the shrill of their long-ago guns
Which still pierce the morning chill.
I lift my head to search for the scent of
Acrid cordite, as it eases
Away from hot breech and barrel.
But it too eludes, drifted that day
On that same summer wind
That carried your ashes away.

I wipe the red rust,
As it runs with the morning dew,
Like tears on a dirty face - my face.
Rust of burned cars,
So many sewing machines,
So many melted, twisted things,
Deformed in their dying, writhing agony.
Charred blackness replaced
By enduring rust.

I stand where your killers stood and
Look into the church at your anxious faces.
Would they have dared look into your eyes?
Where were the brave soldiers that day?
Did they stay away?
They forever marred these sacred walls,
Stones never meant for guns, innocent blood.
My hands trace the deep scars,
My fingers too small to fill their depth.
Angry holes left by those who came to kill.

I see your fear and turn away
When your ghosts look my way.
In the church, crammed together,
You clutch your children here, there.
Cling to each other. You are safe here,
Not yet afraid enough to pray.
But when you do, you will not finish.
Men spew their horror, their hate,
And the cross is too high to reach.

All ask why. But the why remains.
Gone are the six hundred forty-two,
Not one Jew. Their millions dead elsewhere,
Where, like here, there was no mercy
Once the merciless filled their streets.
And where do murderers go
When their work is finished?

They slink away like mongrel dogs,
And disappear into the years.

Balloons from Gaza

They floated in from the South
When the wind was right.
Gifts from Hamas boys:
Colorful kites and
Balloons from Gaza.

We ran to catch them,
Pink, yellow, blue, but
All with strange tails, too.
Then our squeals became anguished appeals
When the balloons set things ablaze
And we ran home
To watch our fields and forests burn.

Benjamin ran to a colorful balloon
With a strange tail
And suddenly disappeared like magic.
We saw his mother cry,
But didn't know why.
It was only a balloon he wanted
To play with for a while.

Then we learned a new song,
A new poem, too,
Which told us what to do
When the wind was right
And the Hamas boys
Could send us kites and gay
Balloons from Gaza.

They say it will be a decade
Before the fields and forests heal;
And Benjamin will not come home.
In a decade I'll be older than the Hamas boys
Who sent us the kites and balloons,
And I will know why they made them
Do things they aren't supposed to do.

And then I will know, too,
Why those strange machines
Instead of me and Benjamin,
Were made to play with the kites
And Balloons from Gaza.

The Charge of the Light Brigade

By Alfred, Lord Tennyson

I

Half a league, half a league,
Half a league onward,
All in the valley of Death
Rode the six hundred.
"Forward, the Light Brigade!
Charge for the guns!" he said.
Into the valley of Death
Rode the six hundred.

II

"Forward, the Light Brigade!"
Was there a man dismayed?
Not though the soldier knew
  Someone had blundered.
  Theirs not to make reply,
  Theirs not to reason why,
  Theirs but to do and die.
  Into the valley of Death
  Rode the six hundred.

III

Cannon to right of them,
Cannon to left of them,
Cannon in front of them
  Volleyed and thundered;
Stormed at with shot and shell,
Boldly they rode and well,
Into the jaws of Death,
Into the mouth of hell
  Rode the six hundred.

IV

Flashed all their sabres bare,
Flashed as they turned in air
Sabring the gunners there,
Charging an army, while
  All the world wondered.
Plunged in the battery-smoke
Right through the line they broke;
Cossack and Russian
Reeled from the sabre stroke
  Shattered and sundered.
Then they rode back, but not
  Not the six hundred.

V

Cannon to right of them,
Cannon to left of them,
Cannon behind them
　Volleyed and thundered;
Stormed at with shot and shell,
While horse and hero fell.
They that had fought so well
Came through the jaws of Death,
Back from the mouth of hell,
All that was left of them,
　Left of six hundred.

VI

When can their glory fade?
O the wild charge they made!
　All the world wondered.
Honour the charge they made!
Honour the Light Brigade,
　Noble six hundred!

Death in the Quakies

It's cold here in the Quakies,
Quiet. Deep snow absorbs
The wind rattle of leafless limbs,
Muffles my heavy breath, hard earned.

He is here, and I have followed.
His tracks, fresh and clear,
Disappear under my own
As if he never walked, as if
I never stalked him.

He moves without fear.
But with well-deserved caution.
My hands tremble;
Not from the cold steel I carry
But knowing
What will follow.

I saw him before
When the spring muck
Held his large prints and
On safe summer days
When he stood in the clearing;
When there was no need for me
To follow, here in the Quakies.

They are lovely trees, these Quakies.
Begetting groves of green
And a richness of gold
At the proper time.
I marvel at their dead winter coat,
How it contrasts now
With the white virgin blanket
Spread before us.
They will come alive again.
If only he could.

This is not an easy place
For one to end.
But a fine place
For his last view of great beauty,
And to leave an evil world
Which I bring with me
Here in the Quakies.

I see him now
Because he moves,
But the Quakies are in the way.
They make it hard
To see, to move,
To bring him close,
And he is smart and knows
His only chance is here
In the Quakies.

Does he wonder
What evil moves in the shadows?
What pursues like a relentless ghost?
Will he wonder till my crosshairs find him
Here in the Quakies?

Grey Sage

The Muley stood, high up in the cold,
Just below the ridge on the steep slope.
A king in the grey sage.
He could have stayed down, unseen,
But he got up and moved.
They always do
When the sun comes up and
Warms the hillsides.

The does laid still and unseen
Until the shot echoed off the hill
And thundered into the soft snow.
Then they up and ran — stopped,
Looked, ran again.
So many not seen before the shot.

He'd stood bravely as the scope's
Crosshairs found his heart.

Then the climb began
To find him, bring him down.
Grey sage, crushed by hands
That grabbed and pulled
Up the steep hill,
Sweetened the morning air
And cleared away
The lingering scent of cordite.

Then, there, gorgeous gray
As the sage, almost
As noble as before.
But red spread on white snow
And gave the truth away.

Heavy and steep —
There was no gentle descent.
But grey sage broke
The awkward slips and slides,
As a red trail followed
Like breadcrumbs.
But only magpies and coyotes
Went back to what was left.

We lifted him to the edge
Of the white tailgate,
Held there as his blood
Dripped and ran down in rivulets,
Dried quickly, turned black in the cold.
A careless arm smeared it,
Like an artist dismayed
At an imperfect stroke
Or a murderer's mistake.
But it matters not.
Forensics and artists
Are not needed here.

A twig of broken sage
Hooked on an antler point.
His still eyes,
Once clear and bright, now
Death dulled to the color of grey sage.

The Swallow Tails Have Returned

The Swallow tails have arrived.
I saw them today, banking, turning:
Effortless ease in the bright blue.
Eager for their return
I searched the skies for days
With anxious thoughts,
For their visit tells me
Things are normal in the world.
But they've been away.
They could not know.

Spring has arrived, too.
They always bring Spring.
I know they look down
And remember me, as
Familiar as my high pines and
Cypress which skirt the lake
And they much prefer,
For they can gather there
Close together.

They see me now, alone,
As I walk the soft straw-strewn paths
And warm, sandy trails
Through the pines and palmettos.
They must recall last year's visit
When things were different below
And I was with friends.
But they have been away
And do not know.

Graceful, soaring raptors,
Their forked tails signal victory,
Like Churchill, who stood
Resolute in the debris
Of the London Blitz.
Their white breasts and underwings,
Angelic-like against a darkness
Which belies the graceful
Sweep and search
Of a silent hunter.

Pandemic Eyes

Ah, the eyes!
The eyes, aye!
Once the mystic realm of Mecca,
Where niqabs housed
Lovely oval almonds
Exuding mystery, conjuring
Romance in the darkness
 Of vast Arabian deserts.
Our cultures clash,
Our religious divide, deep.
And once we laughed,
Questioned its need.
Now we don our own niqab.

Ah, the eyes!
The eyes, aye!
Once fortified by smiles
Or frowns and tears had
Far to fall with wet trails
To gently wipe away.
Colors did not matter much.
But now they are green fields
And pastures out of reach,
Forbidden blue of foreign skies,
And brown, far-off deserts,
All seen through a new lens,
An obscure optic.

Ah, the eyes!
The eyes, aye!
Once only raptors
Saw so clearly.
But now we see as well,
And a shield cannot hide
What lies behind and deep within
Where we search for those
Soft waters of kindness.
While the windows to our soul
Are laid bare and far brighter,
Far clearer, and cannot
Hide our fears and spears of rage.

The Handshake of 1917

Two soldiers clasp hands:
Worn and frazzled both,
Stained from others blood,
Muddied by saddened fields
Which sag with the weight
Of heavy rains and death
That floods in and around.

1917, the camera moves in
Focused on their powerful grip.
Caked mud and blood shows
Clearly on the backs of
Their hands and sleeves.
One brought news:
"Your brother, slain at the front."

In that swell of death
Their hands conveyed thanks,
And life arced
Between two men
Who could not speak the words
In a place where
Death ruled the day.

A fist bump there would not do.
It would not do what handshakes do.
It cannot do what handshakes do.
We are without them now,
But we will shake hands again.
We must shake hands again.

High Flight
by John Gillespie Magee, Jr.

 Oh! I have slipped the surly bonds of Earth
And danced the skies on laughter-silvered wings.
Sunward I've climbed, and joined the tumbling mirth
Of sun-split clouds, - and done a hundred things
You have not dreamed of –
Wheeled and soared and swung
High in the sunlit silence. Hov'ring there,
I've chased the shouting wind along, and flung
My eager craft through footless halls of air . . .
Up, up the long, delirious burning blue
I've topped the wind-swept heights with easy grace
Where never lark, or ever eagle flew —
And, while with silent, lifting mind I've trod
The high untrespassed sanctity of space,
Put out my hand and touched the face of God.

The Layover

Why does fate tempt so?
She sat too close
Where eyes could meet with ease,
Search and tease.
Why such noble restraint?
Why not an unfaithful rogue?
Could I not keep such betrayal
A secret in my heart?
Or would it be written
Forever in my eyes and in my soul?

A long flight over too soon.
An exit too swift.
Would these be our final words
As we approached her turn?
"Laying over?" she asked.
A "come with me" nod,
An invite, not a question.
Twinkling eyes, eager, alive,
Soft, hungry, a lovely name.
She tapped on my lust.
Intoxicated by curves, scent, sight,
An accent of such delight.

We snaked along
Approached the fork.
Would I go left
Where I should go,

To another long flight
And go on alone again
To some place
Long-forgotten now?

Or go right, tempted so,
To a place never to forget?
Heart quickened, mind raced,
Would she go on alone,
Home alone, disappear forever
As it should be?
Never to see her again,
But in a soft memory,
Late on lonely nights
And many more long flights
Where I would always
Look for her again.
Long for her scent,
Her voice in every accent.

Pensive

The dappled grey stood tall,
A proud gelding in his stall,
Head high and out the half-door.
Anxious eyes, nostrils flared,
He stomped and pawed the floor.
Ears erect, he searched the source
Of the leathery squeak
Of tack and saddle
And subtle clang of
Stirrup and bridle
That moved with the rhythmic
Steps of a young rider.

The boy mucked the stall,
Leaned against the wall,
Then worked the new hay
As earthy smells of equine sweat
And urine rose in the humid day.
He felt his work.
Calloused hands
Pulled knots and burrs gently
From the coarse mane
While girlish grunts approached and
His shy eyes waited in vain
As she struggled with the
Heavy weight of tack.

The grey, brushed down well,
Swished and snapped his long, free tail
At biting flies.
Relentless in the crowded stall, they
Clustered round his moist eyes.
He thought of her
As she approached, his
Head high to sniff the air,
Search it like the grey.
Then she was there.
Her scent filled the stall,
Like good whisky.

He staggered as he breathed her in.
The bit thudded on eager teeth.
The head worked an approving nod,
Then sniffed for things underneath.
Things hidden the boy couldn't see.

Then he watched them go -
Ride off into the hot day.
Her boots glistened in the sun,
Hair coiffed and tucked;
It needed little to fall
On slender shoulders, on him.
Her khaki riding pants were tight.
Tight.
Sweetly rhythmic with her western gait
And his fingers gently traced
The outline *Pensive* on the nameplate,
Hung at the top of the stall's half-door.

When the Citrus Blooms

I think of you when the citrus blooms
And orange blossoms
Fill the empty lanes between
Endless rows with the sweet scent
That was your perfume.

We rode horses then,
Fast - down the sandy lanes,
I behind you, bareback,
Trying to keep up,
Trying to catch you.
But our horses were unruly.
Yours disliked a saddle,
Refused an English gait
That you knew and wanted so.

I walk those empty rows now
When the citrus blooms.
Your scent fills my soul
As it filled my heart so long ago
When it flashed over your skin,
And every inch of it I explored,
Inhaled deeply as if
I would breathe you forever.

Between the sweetness of the trees
We rode, thundered
And exhausted the unbridled
Strength beneath us.

In a Kiwi Market

I go back often
To that Kiwi market by the wharf,
Where those sweet eyes met mine
And I bought a few of her wares
For no reason but
To linger longer, hoping to find
The right words.
But smiles and eyes were enough
As the evening sun hung long
In the western sky and held up
The Southern Cross debut,
Which I longed to see
But suddenly forgot
When she asked
Why I was there.

Thoughts raced.
How I would move there?
Leave all I knew?
All I had?
Just to wake each morning
To that kind smile,
And find sleep so sweet?
Once those lovely eyes
Were the final frame
Of the day and
Dreams engulfed my night,
And the southern hemisphere

Wrapped its warm, welcoming arms
Around my weariness as
Fletcher Christian whispered
Seductive suggestions in my ear.

It was but a brief breath of a moment
Which hung with me far longer
Than any photograph could do.
And I go back to that Kiwi market
By the wharf often and wonder
Why I did not obey Fletcher
And buy all those things
Which would have
Kept me there longer.

Like My Red Toyota

She set my head spinning
As she gleamed in the morning sun,
Hypnotized me in the afternoon.
Night lit, she was a runway model.
I lingered like Tom Sawyer
At Becky's fence. Hoping
She was meant for me one day,
To take me away
To places where no one else would,
No one else could.

Hood straps meant only for me
To unsnap, gently, but determined
To explore underneath
With experienced hands
Meant only for her:
To sooth, heal all bangs and bruises,
Bind up wounds from our long
Romantic desert trek.

Dry her gently,
After we'd crossed swollen,
Crock-infested streams
On vast African plains.
Attach something loose,
Rocked and knocked about
On a rough mountain pass;

Drive into an angry wind,
Weather storms,
When she would press on, undeterred
As others failed, afraid, lacked desire,
Content to turn and rest roadside.

Then…

The big, black Rolls pulled up
Beside me at the light;
I looked down into open seats
Where she alone drove and
Smiled up at me, a "follow-me" smile!
A car unlike all others
Driven by one as lovely
As that new day was.
Red hair,
Like rare copper in the morning sun,
She set my head spinning, too,
Just like my red Toyota.

But she turned
Down a street I could not follow
And disappeared into the
Cavernous remembrances
Of my dreams, where she remains
Parked alongside my red Toyota.

If

By Rudyard Kipling

If you can keep your head when all about you
    Are losing theirs and blaming it on you,
If you can trust yourself when all men doubt you,
    But make allowance for their doubting too;
If you can wait and not be tired by waiting,
    Or being lied about, don't deal in lies,
Or being hated, don't give way to hating,
    And yet don't look too good, nor talk too wise:

If you can dream — and not make dreams your master;
    If you can think — and not make thoughts your aim;
If you can meet with Triumph and Disaster
    And treat those two impostors just the same;
If you can bear to hear the truth you've spoken
    Twisted by knaves to make a trap for fools,
Or watch the things you gave your life to, broken,
And stoop and build 'em up with worn-out tools:

If you can make one heap of all your winnings
    And risk it on one turn of pitch-and-toss,
And lose, and start again at your beginnings
    And never breathe a word about your loss;
If you can force your heart and nerve and sinew
    To serve your turn long after they are gone,
And so hold on when there is nothing in you
    Except the Will which says to them: 'Hold on!'
If you can talk with crowds and keep your virtue,

Or walk with Kings—nor lose the common touch,
If neither foes nor loving friends can hurt you,
  If all men count with you, but none too much;
If you can fill the unforgiving minute
  With sixty seconds' worth of distance run,
Yours is the Earth and everything that's in it,
  And—which is more—you'll be a Man, my son!

Seven Glass Panels of Light

She cut seven holes in the roof,
Filled the ceiling with glass
To let the light in,
Allow the sun to warm the floor.
Who would do such a thing?
Some mocked, criticized, questioned.
"How odd" they whispered.
Maybe a skylight, but seven holes?

Then they all looked up
When the sun lit the winter room
Filtered clean by bare trees above.
They moved to the warm rays,
Secretly wished they had courage
To do such an odd thing.
They marveled at the moon
Framed seven times overhead.
It cast their shadows
Ghost-like on tables, chairs, walls,
And stars, too, appeared on cold nights
When skies were clear and bright.

And then white contrails framed in the high blue,
Like footprints in sand before the next wave.
Birds bounced on limbs,
Their white droppings dabbed the glass
Then washed away in a lovely white rivulet
When the rains came.

Winds shook the hickory nuts loose
To smack like gun shots and
Break panels here, there, and hail, too.
But glass is easy to replace
For a view of space and
Far off heat lightning hiding in high clouds
As fire-flies filled the void between flashes.

Turn out the lights and watch them work.
Sit in the big rocking chair and look up
Through the seven panels at life.
You'll not see through a roof
With no holes
And your lack of courage
To see beyond the boundaries
Of your fears and hesitations.

But time collected on the glass,
Etched it cloudy, and
Fall leaves put away their finest and
Left their limbs to dance and fall
And lie still on the glass with old
Spring buds who'd done their work, too.
Mold found a foothold.
Mildew grew and soon
There were new cracks and leaks
And the glass was hard to reach.
Then the rainbows were gone.
The pink clouds of sunsets

Were memories and snowflakes
Melted to water and
Fattened the black stagnant mass
That covered the glass
And the squirrels could only
Be heard as they danced
A sad, slow waltz across
The dark panels above.

But the panels shone bright for a while,
Lit up and warmed the room for a short spell-
Made others marvel at what could be
If one dares imagine a sky seen
Through a roof with seven glass panels.

Where Da Moss Don't Grow

Oh, I cain't live where da moss don't grow.
It be too cold and sometime it might snow.
Da cypress and oak gotta look old and grey,
And in da wind, gotta whisper and sway.

Some Yankee say he don't like da moss.
Say it block da sun, that da light be lost.
But I cain't live where da moss don't grow.
I like it hangin' round where da black water flow.

Sometime I walk barefoot down dat cool sand road,
Through da tunnel of oak, carryin' my load.
Dat moss be swaying, and I be thinkin' bout my girl,
And dat moss be flowing like her long dark curl.

And in da Spring when da 'zalia
Blaze round da trunk,
I pick dat pink blossom and wid a kiss jus' fo' luck,
Place it in dat grey flowing moss and curl,
And know I'm richer than diamond and pearl.

Now my sista say dat moss be da beards
Of all them dead rebels them Yankees feared.
Say they gotta hang forever for all to see
Dat them rebel spirits still roam free.

But Mama say dat ain't right,
Say da moon weave dat moss on a cold, dark night,
When da wind blow hard from out da north,
And da riva rise up and fear come forth.

Say da moon weave dat moss
For a lost Seminole child
Whose mama climbed da high cypress
And cried aloud,
To dat storm fo mercy
On her child so young.
So da moon weave dat moss
While dat hurricane sung.

Now dat child was spared, kept safe thru da night,
While in dat moss wrapped warm and tight.
Then dat moon come out, see da work of his hand,
And so pleased, spread dat moss
Cross his favored land.

So, I won't live where dat moss don't grow.
I like it hangin' round me in this ole boat I row.
I like da way it dress up da pine.
I like dat moss, I like it jus' fine.

The Old Chair

The old chair was not allowed in the house.
Unwelcome, it lacked class and didn't match:
Too old, worn, sun-bleach faded,
Like old skin, long in the sun.
No one knew where it came from
Or when it arrived. It'd just been around-
Showed up like an old stray dog
Needing a friendly pat on the back.

I took it out to the pasture,
A sturdy seat to shoot from.
Left it there through the winter,
Till spring grass grew through it.
Then a good chair was needed at the barn
To help watch over newborn calves,
Rest a tired back after a long day in the field,
Sip whisky in the evening, smoke a slow cigar.

It sat good by the night fire
Where rough men told stories
And it heard things that
Maybe it shouldn't have.
But it kept secrets.
And it was a good place to sit and
Listen to the dogs run at night,
Then watch the sun rise or set.
And it didn't mind a little tobacco spit.

Or black coffee spilt from calloused hands
That once made it peg-tight.
But the seat was split bad,
Like a deep scar across a young cheek.
And old paint from a more glorious life
Still clung in grooves, ever hopeful
For a fresh coat that'll never come.
Paint don't work where there's work to be done.

A chair inside don't live much.
It don't carry scars by errant knives or
Legs gnawed on by generations of dogs,
Or befriend a nearby deer stand.
It won't see the hay grow,
Get cut, teddered, and bailed.
An inside chair just won't work outside.
The old chair will.
Just needs a pat on the back.

Under the Kudzu

Flowing mounds of green
Blanket like snow,
Soften the edge
Of sharp limb, broken barn,
A long dead tractor.

Beneath the green
Vines: creeping, gaining,
Winning, till winter's victory,
When dead and grey,
It backs away,
Lies down with the cold
And waits
For another spring,
Another summer's assault.

Laughed at, mocked, but
Still there, everywhere.
Underneath, a mottled,
Sunlit world, unseen
To passersby who
Tsk! Tsk! and claim
The shame of it. So wild,
Untamed, what can be done?

Under the kudzu
We stay. We play.
We tunnel here, there.

We know what lies beneath
This green blanket
Thrown over our world.

We see beyond the vines
Hiding our peering eyes.
But you, now grown,
Weighted with what
Years bring, have forgotten
Our tunnels here, our world,
Under the kudzu.

A kiss, long ago
Set two hearts aflutter.
Two who flew
So far apart.
But the kudzu returns,
Green, lush, flowing,
Hiding what lies beneath
Our made-up world,
Our unfinished promise,
A remembered kiss,
Under the kudzu.

Uncle Morris

The old plantation house sat crooked,
Sagged to one side like
Uncle Morris carrying a heavy cotton sack.
Lonely, too, sitting way up back
Beyond the long cotton field,
Green sometimes, then white
When the cotton opened,
Like it snowed early.
Big angry machines picked it then,
Left the field dark,
Shaved down to start over.

That's when they all came,
Gathered round the old house.
The dogs and guns came out,
Corn piles grew in front of tree stands.
Then the old house breathed again,
Its warm breath exhaled out the chimney.
Mornings smelled of coffee and bacon,
Mixed with kitchen wood smoke.
At night its lights looked out without envy
On the darkness and cold, barren fields.

Dogs shivered in the yard.
Uncle Morris wasn't there
As cigar smoke swirled round back rooms
And dark whiskey filled glass after glass,
Fortified courage, loosened tongues.

He came next day.
His large granddaughter brought him by.
He sat regal-like in his old pickup
Which shook all over
Like her when she laughed.

"Ya'll ain't neva do no huntin' upyea," he said.
"Ya'll jus upyea drinkin' an carrinon.
Whes all ya'lls women folk?"
Her body shook, head rocked in mock shame.
He put his hundred-year-old hand on mine,
Pinned it to the door,
Black as low country soil: warm and kind.
"I sees ya dis evenin." he grinned and winked.
"Ya'll gots ta git ya sum sportin' womens upyea."

It was a calloused hand, worked hard a century.
He was a tall Masai warrior, a wise Kukuyu Chief.
That evening he sat by the fire like a Zulu King,
His white subjects gathered round the flames.
Sparks danced, disappeared into the blackness,
Flickered in his old eyes, still and calm,
An old African lion looking down on the plains
From a high hill, dreaming of younger days,
Of prides and hunts he'd once led.
He stood up.

Tall and dark as the night,
One lone, old, black man surrounded by white,
Like a thick cotton field ready for picking.
It grew still, quiet, a log shifted, flames whispered.

Then he gave a hundred-year-old Lord's Prayer
Filled with spirits, pain, life, strife.
Words that should be in the Bible,
Should be captured, should be kept.
But they drifted off with the smoke
Into the quiet night.

The white men held their hats, reverent.
Bowed their heads, eyes closed.
Then ghosts of their ancestors
Got up, danced round the flames
Spoke to them, for them.
They spoke of revolution, the King's tax.
Argued secession, state's rights, cotton, slavery.
Drank moonshine, defied prohibition.
Heads hung low, out of work.
They cursed Nazis, Japs, Yankees and Jews.

Their ghosts spat in the fire.
It hissed at the words of integration.
Then one yelled for a tree and a rope.
All dressed in white,
As white as the heavy cotton field
Before the angry machines did their work.

The Road Not Taken
By Robert Frost

Two roads diverged in a yellow wood,
And sorry I could not travel both
And be one traveler, long I stood
And looked down one as far as I could
To where it bent in the undergrowth;

Then took the other, as just as fair,
And having perhaps the better claim,
Because it was grassy and wanted wear;
Though as for that the passing there
Had worn them really about the same,

And both that morning equally lay
In leaves no step had trodden black.
Oh, I kept the first for another day!
Yet knowing how way leads on to way,
I doubted if I should ever come back.

I shall be telling this with a sigh
Somewhere ages and ages hence:
Two roads diverged in a wood, and I—
I took the one less traveled by,
And that has made all the difference.

Still

Winter's tight-fisted grip
Still opens early
For the daffodils to sing.

And grey-stubbled locust posts
Still guard their eternal line
In the uncut pasture grass.

And deep-throated feral dogs
Still send their warnings
From nearby wooded hills.

And lonely night trains
Still follow and leave
Their same unchanged track.

And the rebuilt church
Still rings out to seduce young souls
And soothe the old.

And eager spring buds
Still open bright to teach
The bees to hum in tune.

And children's laughter
Still tinkles in the hollows
Like crystal wind chimes in the wind.

And naughty, evening shadows
Still creep silently up the hill
To sleep with the night.

And the coughing tractor
Still intrudes the quiet
From the old road above the creek.

And anxious young faces
Still look out and frown
From behind fog breathed glass.

And the hard spring rains
Still push the creek
To defy the bank's rule.

And lofty, lazy buzzards
Still circle in the high blue above,
Eager for what lies below.

And the hungry woodpecker
Still drums his dinner
On dead limbs and hollow trunks.

And neighbor cows
Still bellow resentment
But happy for warm sun on their hide.

And arrogant crows
Still strut and caw as they
Search the field for forgotten corn.

And the smell of new cut hay
Still mixes with cedar and pine,
A sweet fragrance of an afternoon gin.

And the proud box woods
Still guard invisible porch steps,
Seen only in a ghostly photograph.

And thick old oaks
Still stand firm and stoic
Forever silent to their witness.

And the mist eases up from the creek
Still play-acting as smoke to tease and
Swirl around a crumbled chimney.

And steaming, morning coffee
Still fills the day with promise while
Waited for in the fading dark.

And angry logger trucks
Still growl in the distance
As they gear down the steep grade.

And old bricks and hearth stones
Still demand to be seen
But cannot escape summer's vines.

And the smiling grey fox
Still jumps for mice
In the heavy pasture grass,

And the shy whitetail
Still sneeze in the thickets
Unseen until they move.

And all their ghosts walk beside me
Still
Down the evening's long dirt road.

Odd Inspiration

They inspired me:
A cigar, a beer and a bag of chips.
Under the tall palm by the lake
I sat, watched the night come in
When there was no wind
And the dog lay at my feet;
I stuck a toe under her
Where it was soft and warm
And waited for the first star.
Always the bright one in the west
Leads the way and then the shy ones
Come out to play as the lake glimmered
Like glass while lights from homes
Glanced off the mirrored water,
So still, I could not tell
Which were real.

A glow from the slow cigar
Smiled, so I kept the ash,
Let it grow before it fell
Into the abalone shell
Which glimmered, too,
But not like it used to
When first pulled from the sea.
Then my patient hand searched
In the dark for hiding chips,
Those remaining few as
I spat tobacco flakes,

Which I do well (and like to do),
While the bottle
Sweats and wets its coat.
I wiped the running rows
From its brow. It thanked me;
It thanked me somehow.

I breathed life into the glow
And slowly killed the beer.
Funny how one thing dies
And another doesn't live
Until it burns its way to an end
And cannot live without a friend
Who burdens the air with smoke.

We were all friends there for a while:
One, a warm, red glow I got to know
Another, liquid gold I would not share,
The third settled the score.
But time was short as night fell.
Then the empty bag exhaled and fell.
The bottle drained dry like an empty well,
A wetted end of what remained,
I crushed into the shell with heartless ease
And sparks ran from me into the lifting breeze.

Comanche Dream

Bareback on painted ponies
We cross the clear, cold stream.
Ahead the tall grass beacons,
But dark skies where we have been.

We stop to water ponies
And breathe the free-scented wind.
Ahead blue skies call us
But they are dark where we have been.

Loose stones beneath our ponies' hooves
Chant "Farewell O'Faithful Friends."
Clear waters cool our heated blood
Now dark where we have been.

Ahead my brothers climb the bank,
Our ponies eager for the run.
Behind us lies a long dark night,
Our land without our sun.

Dust kicked up by eager hooves
Is the scent of sweet, rich earth.
We breathed this for a thousand years,
Long before this strange new birth.

We once rode to war; we rode to hunt;
We rode for freedom's thrill.
But a new spirit calls us now,
To a new light beyond the hill.

Bareback on painted ponies
We cross the clear, cold stream.
Ahead the tall grass beckons,
But forever dark where we have been.

A Red-Tail's Late Arrival

The field was neatly cut.
My work nearly done.
But he knew the sound well
And quite far he'd come.
He'd stand watch in the oak,
Shredded now in the wind.
I forgave his late arrival,
Eager for him to begin.

He kept his eye on me,
His only friend this day.
So, I cut the field with care
As the rabbits and mice ran away.
But they'd not go far in the cold,
Nor all escape my indifferent blade.
They'd now nowhere to lay,
Nor his eye could they evade.

He stood long at attention,
Pruned a salute quite well.
He was patient for me to finish,
Eager to work as well.
And now my field fell silent.
My blade had done its job.
Then I looked at the rows of trenches
And all those I had robbed.

Outlived and Outworked

Old locust wood fence posts never rot,
As long as they stand upright and hold fast
To their four-strand wire
Meant to keep the cows in.

Some bend a little from the wind over time,
And honeysuckle will creep up and lay heavy
On the wire, while selfish cedars
Claim favored fence corners,
Grow tall and fat, with full skirts
That hide their thick-ankled trunks
As they dance with the pasture grass.

Deer go over, dogs under.
Both leave hair on the wire.
Scrub trees snake up between the wires and
Cut deep into trunks that bleed
Sap from scars that never heal.

Winter frost first whitens then wets
Rusty wires when the sun comes up to
Shave frost stubble from old gray post tops.
Polk berries thrive between posts,
Feed robins till they wobble on the wire
Like sailors on shore leave.

The men who long ago
Put these posts in the ground now rest there, too.
The posts outlived and outworked them all.
It's good to clear old locust wood
Fence lines now and then,
Even if the cows are gone and
The old house has fallen in.
The wire might sag a long, shy smile of thanks
As it hides deep in blackberry thorns.

So, rest your tired elbow on an old locust post
Tight in the hard ground and maybe
Bent a little from the wind, but still at work.
Feel its strength and know
It'll outlast and outwork you
As long as it stands upright and holds fast
To its four-strand wire.

Sea Fever
by John Mansfield

I must go down to the sea again,
to the lonely sea and the sky,
And all I ask is a tall ship and a star to steer her by,
And the wheel's kick and the wind's song
And the white sail's shaking,
And a grey mist on the sea's face,
And a grey dawn breaking.

I must down to the sea again,
for the call of the running tide
Is a wild call and a clear call that may not be denied;
And all I ask is a windy day
with the white clouds flying,
And the flung spray and the blown spume,
and the seagulls crying.

I must down to the sea again,
to the vagrant gypsy life,
To the gull's way and the whale's way
where the wind's like a whetted knife.
And all I ask is a merry yarn
from a laughing fellow-rover,
And a quiet sleep and a sweet dream
when the long trip's over.

Breath of the St. Johns

Her breath, my first.
Brackish brine, sulfuric, and thick.
Pressed on my senses,
Implanted on my soul.
My infant milk,
To suckle a lifetime.

In distant lands, in future years,
I long for her.
I know her there, everywhere.
Wherever heat sears
Or cold numbs all thought
But one, of her.

I know her well.
She laced my discontent
With her contrary flow
So oddly north.
Still, she carries me
Seaward, ever seaward.

We gain strength with age,
With each new swelling,
Endless tidal rhythms,
Filling, leaving
Seaward forever,
Always together.

Her jungled banks
Clench tepid waters, tea stained,
Seasoned with palm,
Tanned by pine and palmetto.
A gator garnish
Iced with Ibis down.

Fueled by dark, eager streams
And cold, crystal springs,
Inland born, seaward bound.
Faint fragrance of Spain, of Seminole.
All gifts for me
As we seek the sea.

Seaward, ever seaward.
Where winds rise to smite,
Storms seek the weak,
Where river and sea meet
An ocean is born…
Our breath the same.

A Sparrowhawk and a Dove

I did not see the feathers explode
When he hit like a missile.
I did not hear the last, weak breath
When steel sharp talons struck and clenched.
I expected no quarter nor mercy.
I knew they did not exist, but
Hoped for them, nonetheless.

There was only the swift pursuit,
The determined flee,
The streak of hunter and hunted
Across a blue, happy day,
A steady, quiet closing, gaining
The other — failing
To outwit, outmaneuver, outlive.

On such a fine day
How did one find the other
So unlucky?
One was to sit on my roof's eave
And coo softly in the afternoon.
The other to circle, glide, and
Be admired in his high majestic hunt.

Before You Go

Lie here awhile before you go
Through the night now, still and close,
Where our eyes can meet with ease
And think on days of greater strength and speed.

Ravaged now, weak, and gaunt,
Your life light fades before me.
Your labored breath no more from
Golden fields and forest runs.

Why can I not renew your sinewy strength,
Your fiery eyes?
Why can it not be so?
Why must you go?

Rise and run with me again,
Hunt with me once more before you go.
Sound your faithful, night alarm.
I slept well with you near and feared no harm.

Your collar now loose and limp,
Once strained with swelled strength and pride.
Why must one so faithful suffer so?
Let's run again the fields before you go.

Lie here awhile before you go.

My Diamonds

Countless diamonds drop outside
From the arm of an old oak.
Morning light sets them afire.
They are flawless, clear, perfectly cut.
Bright blues and veiled rainbows spit
From their precious moments.
They are rare as the Millennium Star,
The Centenary, and they are mine alone,
My April, Sixty-year moment and Hope.
Each my heraldry and armorial bearing.

They are not carbon born,
Pressed from millennia coal,
Nor dug from deep, African mines
Washed in mud and blood,
Not shipped and sold in a De Beers world
Or used to cut steel.
None glitter on elegant necks, adorn sleek fingers,
Accentuate ears, or attract store-front crowds
To impress and amaze under lit glass.
These are not longed for by the yet-engaged
Nor secure in thick-walled vaults or
Displayed in museums, lit like July fireworks.
The nefarious have no chance to plan their theft.

They are simple remnants of a night's rain
Fermented in Plato's Stars.
They drop, replaced in kind.
I mine their brilliance,
Determine their carat, clarity, and color.
But have only a moment to do so
Before sun and gravity steal them and
Morning light and rain
Refuse to ever rightly align again.
But it is a moment when all
Are my diamonds.

Norman

He stares at me from his book cover,
Standing watch over his oeuvre.
I fear his eyes say, "Give up,
You cannot master it as I have."
But he was a teacher
And would not say that.

His cigarette clings precariously
Between two fingers like
A free climber hanging one-armed
Over the high edge of life.

His ash will never drop,
But I want him to thump it,
Then breath in deeper
So the end will flare and
Glow bright again
And free his hand to write.

Maybe then he would say,
"Come on, get with it.
Find your own Assynt."

About the Author

Michael is a former Naval Officer and Navy SEAL who served over twenty-six years on active duty. He was awarded a Bronze Star during Desert Storm and numerous other personal awards during a long and illustrious career.

Following retirement as a Navy Captain, he served eight years as Executive Director of the National Navy SEAL Museum. The 2007 Congressional Record of the 110th Congress records his name and outlines his efforts which significantly improved, expanded, and built the nation's only memorial to fallen Navy SEALs. He helped author the legislation, signed by President Bush, for the museum's National Designation.

Influenced early in life by Rudyard Kipling and Alfred, Lord Tennyson, Michael began writing poetry as a cadet at The Citadel where his work first appeared in the school's literary magazine *The Shako*. His long career as a Naval Officer and Navy SEAL provided dramatic life experiences, extensive foreign travel, and the adventures, which now fuel his work.

Michael was a 2015, 2017, and 2021 Poetry Finalist in the Florida Writers Association's Royal Palm Literary Awards and a Bronze winner in 2021. His work appeared in the 2018 Indian River State College Journal *The Indian River Review*, the 2018 and 2019 Laura Riding Jackson Foundation's (LRJF) "Porch Writers" chapbooks, and the 2022 chapbook "Musings on the Art of Eldon Lux." He presently leads the LRJF's Pole Barn Poets writer group.

Michael's thought-provoking columns have appeared in the San Diego, California, Virginia Beach, Virginia, and local Treasure Coast newspapers. He appeared on TV productions for the History Chanel, Military Chanel and Weaponology, as well as numerous local and state news, tourism and documentary productions. For several years he wrote for *Main Street Focus Magazine*, coached high school soccer, and caught wild dolphins in the Indian River Lagoon for health assessment studies by the Georgia Aquarium.

Notes

"My Dhow"
Finalist and Bronze Award 2021 – Florida Writers Association (FWA), Royal Palm Literary Awards (RPLA)
A Dhow under sail at sea is the loveliest of seafaring vessels. Endemic to the Arab coastlines, their beautiful lines and history captured my imagination. I often dreamed of bringing one home to sail our Atlantic coastline.

"High in the Hindu Kush"
This poem refers to Operation Red Wings, a 2005 operation in Afghanistan when 11 SEALs were killed on one operation making it the single greatest loss of Navy SEAL lives at any one moment in all of SEAL history. (Tragically, this number would be eclipsed in 2011.) It was sudden, tragic, and sad. I didn't know any of these fine young men but in essence, I knew them all. We had a common bond, the brotherhood. There but for the grace of God go I. The movie and book *Lone Survivor* will add further context.

"Rock of Remagen"
Finalist 2017 - Florida Writers Association (FWA), Royal Palm Literary Awards (RPLA)
I grew up just outside Fort Jackson in Columbia, South Carolina, so close I could hear the bugles playing reveille and taps. Lovely music indeed. During a recent visit, I took a nostalgic drive around the fort and stopped at a small museum tucked away off the beaten path. There, among tanks and other large war memorability, was a large, strange rock. A closer look told me it was from a strategic bridge where a major battle took place in WWII. Lonely and unassuming, it had so much to say but had no audience.

"A Walk Through Oradour"

Towards the end of WWII, the Nazis rounded up all occupants in the French village of Oradour-sur-Glane and murdered 642 men, women, and children. Some were shot inside the village church. These were not innocent Jews murdered as part of the final solution rather innocent French citizens. After these coldblooded murders, the Nazis destroyed the village. When the war ended French President, Charles de Gaulle, ordered the ruins of the village remain as a memorial and museum. A walk through Oradour today is a walk through it in 1944. It is a sad and sobering experience.

"Balloons from Gaza"

Semi-Finalist 2020 – Florida Writers
Association (FWA), Royal Palm Literary Awards (RPLA)
The terrorist group Hamas used colorful balloons and kites with incendiary ordnance disguised as toys hanging below them to kill and injure innocent Israeli children and set fire to Israeli crops and fields. A people's hate must be unmeasurable to devise such ways to kill and maim their fellow man and target innocent children.

"Death in the Quakies"
"Grey Sage"

The above two poems are reflections of challenging hunts in the wilds of Wyoming, a state I have grown to love.

"The Swallow-Tails Have Returned"
"Pandemic Eyes" Semi-Finalist 2021 FWA
"The Handshake of 1917"

The above three poems are about the pandemic. A comparison of sorts makes reference to Islamic face veils and our covid masks. Reference is also made to a poignant scene in the WWI movie *1917*.

"The Layover"
Purely romantic imagination

"Pensive"
"When the Citrus Blooms"
Semi-finalist 2021 – Florida Writers Association (FWA), Royal Palm Literary Awards (RPLA)
The above two poems reflect on a doomed first love.

"In a Kiwi Market"
More romantic imagination.

"Like My Red Toyota"
My first true love was a shiny, new red Toyota Landcruiser. It sat on display outside the dealership I passed twice daily walking to and from Junior High School. I'm still in love with it and the mysterious copper-haired beauty who drove the Rolls Convertible.

"Seven Glass Panels of Light"
This is for and about my mother. She was a pistol. This is but the tip of the iceberg.

"Where Da Moss Don't Grow"
Who doesn't love the lovely, ghostly, and romantic Spanish Moss? I can't help but marvel at the beauty of this Southern icon. Now you know its origin.

"The Old Chair"
It is what it is: an old friend on our farm.

"Under the Kudzu"

Kudzu, the scourge of the South, invasive, hated by many yet amazing in its aggressiveness and resilience. Originally imported as an ornamental plant and to impede soil erosion, it is now well established as a pest with the ability to spread faster than covid. But I'm rather fond of it, and there's a magical world under its sea of green in summer.

"Uncle Morris"

This is a true story embellished with a bit of imagination. I was honored to meet Uncle Morris years ago while hunting at an old South Carolina plantation. He passed shortly thereafter at an age of over a century. The contrast and irony of his exalted position (well-deserved, I might add) among expansive white cotton fields, and the old plantation surrounded by many white men, was a fascinating and lovely experience.

"Still"

Finalist 2021 – Florida Writers Association (FWA), Royal Palm Literary Awards (RPLA)

I feel this when I walk the dirt roads of our farm, past the ruins of the house my great-grandfather built and where my grandmother and her many sisters and brothers were born. It is a sacred place full of friendly and loving spirits.

"Odd Inspiration"

There is nothing better than sitting in the evening with a cold beer, smoking a fine cigar, with sleeping dogs at my feet.

"Comanche Dream"

This is about the clearest, most colorful, most exhilarating, and realistic dream I've ever experienced. It was a feeling of total freedom, and I woke up reaching for my pony's bridle.

"A Red-Tail's Late Arrival"
This was inspired by a Red-Tailed Hawk who waited patiently for his dinner in a nearby tree while I finished bushhogging a field.

"Outlived and Outworked"
There are countless locust wood fence posts on our North Carolina farm. We can only speculate as to who put them in the ground, but they've easily been there well over a century. They remind me of my Scotch-Irish ancestors who settled, cleared, and farmed this land and their toughness and self-reliance.

"Breath of the St. Johns"
I was born on the banks of the St. Johns River near Jacksonville, Florida, where I have always felt a special connection to that massive, dark-flowing river. This river intrigues me with her mystical and mysterious ways.

"A Sparrowhawk and a Dove"
If you've ever seen a bird of prey at work, you couldn't help but marvel at its intensity of purpose, focus, and cold indifference. They are brilliant.

"Before You Go"
A tribute to my lovely Lady, our beautiful Fox Red Labrador Retriever, who touched my soul deeply for fifteen years. Not a day goes by that I don't reach down beside the bed each morning to gently squeeze her soft muzzle and stroke her noble head. My heart still aches when she's not there.

"My Diamonds"
Inspired by a lovely morning on our farm after a heavy night's rain and a magical sunrise.

"Norman"

The late Norman MacCaig, my favorite Scottish poet, looks at me from the cover of his collection, his oeuvre. He speaks to me.

www.ingramcontent.com/pod-product-compliance
Lightning Source LLC
Chambersburg PA
CBHW031538040426
42445CB00010B/604